GW01237610

Come

Michael Thomas

Oversteps Books

First published in 2014 by

Oversteps Books Ltd
6 Halwell House
South Pool
Nr Kingsbridge
Devon
TQ7 2RX
UK

www.overstepsbooks.com

Copyright © 2014 Michael Thomas
ISBN 978-1-906856-50-2

Printed in Great Britain by imprint digital, Devon

Again to Lynda

Acknowledgements:

Thanks to the following in which some of these poems first appeared: The Cannon's Mouth, Iota, London Grip, Other Poetry, Pennine Platform, Poetry Salzburg Review, Sarasvati, Under the Radar, We're All in This Together (Offa's Press anthology) and Weyfarers.

Contents

Lake

Swans chaperone their majesty,
haul sun-shells in their wake,
tune the grace of entrance
through invisible arches.

Moorhens fare out to willow islands,
warm the farers of the coming year
on lying-in beds
hulled miraculous from dross and switch.

At the edge,
black apples vibrate into coots
who skip and zag
like gabardine men dodging rain,
who topple in, tiny drunks
assured that each fall has its pillow.

Their splashes
rouse the lake to its dimensions,
thread bank to bank
in echoes like a secret name
told once and tucked away
as a feather might fold
in a swan's colossal shade
when the miles drum into its heart,
when it spreads upon the screes of wind
and beats down the world.

Black Countries

Daisy Bank

Coseley, 1961

Daisy Bank
was an hour no day would admit to

a scuttle-through
between the big roads
with their iron ribs and gawpable collisions

cats would go there
to be left out in the rain

old girls, bred among the fiery holes
would miss buses along its perimeter

set down their despairs on a smoky wall
beside Home and Colonial baggage

old boys would staff the kerbs
all flapped apart like strutless umbrellas

never quite getting round to cross
spangles of Ypres in their eyes

the burnt-out Elementary
grew helots to be shipped

when destiny bisected time
about the business of splendour in Limerick or Benin

Princess Mary of Teck stopped there once
a mutton-chop trio was sprung from Beddows' Yard
to re-bore the axle

Perry the Tipton Slasher
finessed his murdering

in the shovel-throws of darkness
behind the Viceroy's Arms.

But a breach of sun
would always find Lane's Electrical

kiss and feather its way
round eight-disc spindles, half-shelled heads

bedizen the skin of Belafonte,
Torme, Ronnie Carroll, Matt Munro

lift their smiles beyond dentition
cherish their hinterlands: Chelsea, Tobago, Bel Air.

Beneath unforecast scraps of blue
Daisy Bank could close its eyes and uncurl

as the songs ascended from Lane's doorway
engaged prefab, triple-chain, exhausted cladding

with forest waters
soda-winks at the uptown hour
stray curls and prodigal lipstick
gondolas rifting the dusk

Mrs Watton

Bilston, 1962

Mrs Watton was quietly, richly there
in our carnival palaver

swathed the borough mornings
with her bump-grille Skoda Octavia

(first in the county, Ben Koczak said,
whose dad dealt in rivers of post-road scrap

and would slow his crusher
to ease the passing of a totalled Bentley)

Mrs Watton's voice
bent down before her head did

no finger ranging imperial
through the scrub of our addled sums, our *e* before *i*

she was that sound-surround disc
you could get them to play you in Hartshorn's —

help singing soft upon your either shoulder
like a child-wind refusing to bulk into a gale

I could give her one, said Paul Day's older brother
leaving us to fathom — cap-gun? dog-daisy?

Mrs Watton was an afternoon
in a week nearing Christmas

we imagined her house, new-build
an estate high above white dogshit

everything mulled and gold about the bricking
the carport filling slowly up

with herald angels working their wings
ready to give it the annual go

swapping tales of the good they'd got up to
all down their shiny twelvemonth

Danny Gallagher finally twigged
which was wattle, which daub

Mrs Watton's voice gentled off
replaced by the Head's door-blasting stride

her words like the plunge of Ben Koczak's dad's crusher:
Gallagher, Day, cigarettes, dead birds

Paul and Danny were fired like rocketless Gagarins
thumped heads on the same display and sank
the flags of a Saxon fastness prinking their curls

Mrs Watton stared, eased them up, slipped out
laid her shadow fleet upon the Head's

did something no-one could say, never ever,
left our brightest year black from Octavia dust

Calls and Responses

Rathkeale
County Limerick

This moment happens like a red leaf
blowing out of mist

in it,
a car full of soured, mid-holiday faces
clips a Georgian corner,
folds a mirror like a ricochet
with no shot to breed it
and jolts off, ancient dusts roused again,
chasing its wings

birds that cannot settle
on the bell-waves that soften the town
make for some secret place, perhaps,
where one of the shining men
laid his cowl and bones to an oak,
slantwise

an old woman, all energy steered
to the fullness of her hands —
the cards, prescriptions —
dies where she stands
from a hole-in-the-wall's shouty brightness —
gets her corpse somehow away
to an alley's last overhang

will we point ye to the hairdresser?
the ringleted tykes shinny down their question,
turn into a shriek of heels,
leave the bald man like burning stone

a lunch-hour boy,
earpiece and pecs and belligerence,
kicks the future down the street
in a shirt of gauleiter blue

the coffee-girl, late,
wakes the afternoon with her breasts
from its little sleeps
dispersed among pearl spigots — with her sigh
in which hope of love is just making to turn
from the last bridge of the parish

next minute, the rain,
smoking where gutters
don't quite meet the flags —
all the sea-hauling clouds
down and thick together
like tipped-off soldiery

Feast of Jude

I wonder if
after all
God is going too

I see him
in a rural vestry
random, mist-braided

coat too heavy for his years
eyes this time unable
to widen enough against the world

blinking fatly
into a chalice's rusty lake
as if they have mislaid their face

out in the hulk of the church
the twilit congregation:

mice with a veldt of sanctity to dart in

organ-pipes hazarding
a note thin as candle-spills
as a winter muse might blow across her fingers

an off-kilter bat
slamming at this or that window
touting the frenzies of hell
all round the outside
in case a skewed latch, a broken diamond
should let them in
to enact the plunge
of the rebel angels
amid the dusts and damps of purity.

God fingers the brim of his hat
he has seen all this too often
huge blocks of disqualified space

like ships with their lights blown out
heeling on the tides of an unfriendly moon.

And elsewhere
beyond the mossing stones of the path
the gate with no anniversaries to test its creak —
all the mad bursts of blood
the flocking along behind blind fairies . . .

. . . and his son in there somewhere
still saying his say

still being bundled out of the ruck
like a fighter whose bones
don't want their pain enough.

God works the ring on the vestry door
forgetting already
that this one is half-right, slow lift, jiggle

his light departs the gaunt adjacencies
somewhere his son cries
the ones about camels and keeping lamps in trim
upends a table weeping gold
in memory of his cadetship

the last of his words
fly up
seeds with no summer
to split in

just the one word
falls back upon the night.

Suffer.

*Jude is the patron saint of lost causes, of 'cases despaired of.' In the western
Christian calendar, his feast day is 28th October. But his appeal extends
beyond the faithful.*

Tintagel

I want to rise in steam
from the leafy thrust
of hot public gardens
and anchor in the skies above Tintagel

where the postmistress
and the lading clerk,
loveless through years of cargo,
of letters insulted by boot-heel and rain,
fall at last in each other's way.

I shall be the promenade
that opens blue
between her corsage and his gravy stains,
the engine of an evening's walk
idling,
the something that aligns her daring toes
with his better-days leather.

I shall, a moment on,
be the pinch-gap
of thumb and finger
lifting ill-chosen pie from his breath
and a lifetime's disabling catch
from hers

so words come
so a murmur outcrooks his elbow
so another hinges her resinous fingers
within it
just so
henceforward.

there's a thing

on a quiet street
at the edge of the town
I met a man holding
a bag upside down

I've dropped the sun
he said
and there it was about his feet
petals and half-shells beating beating
like hearts refused love
refused dreams

he looked a god
who'd never been let past
the middling scree of Olympus
soured gown
bearing lumped and fallen —
a gofer, then, returning the seed of life
prinked and polished and newly fierce
to superiors for upward conveyance

the sky blanched over the roofways
cloud by cloud
it laid off its ecstasies

a moment later
we watched a boy come shuffling up
from the well of the town
crane his neck at the dying frost of stars
the heavens rearing ugly on each other

he looked about to say
well there's a thing
but the air caught up its linens
and we all three fell

the shabby god's cry
at hunks of fire bedding in his face
was the last of pain in the world

Jesus on the strand

1

noon is long over the waves
soon only the stars will be singing

as far as I thought about them
sandals meant getting down into holes
the Sunday world prevented

gammy-legging back up the beach
holding them torn or nubbed with limpets

I didn't think yours
would look like that
don't they hurt?
are you never let off that covenant?

you smooth your clothing
I'd never read or heard that you frown
(or double-take or bridle come to that)

so what is that look in aid of?
perhaps you think of all the words
that take it in turns to infest your cloth
through all your helpless eternity

garb cloak tunic shroud
raiment (for those transports
of dizzying miracle)
and
well
cloth

loin-cloth

what they put on a stick
to drown your bloodied words
was it aspirational vinegar
or plain bad wine?

2

So here you are
and the evening star
fidgets in the high passes

looking for you?
do you pal about together in the dark?
where will you sleep?

there's a village beyond the shingle
one bent street
a handful of life

the usual smorgasbord
probably
of all you came to cry down
saint and sinner prisoned
in the same gabardine or lace

but perhaps also an open shed
a porch window propped against the tease of summer
a dog too tired to rouse the commonwealth

good luck with all that
now I've seen you
I'll try another lost-count time
to remember not to forget

yes that path
up and over the bluff
where that one lamp gulps and fizzes

you're broader than I imagined
do you know anybody with needle and thread?
did you ever get that back seen to?

many mansions

the shepherdess
on the mantel
looks up to heaven

thinks about
the promise of a house
its many mansions

wonders if
there's a mansion for her
at least a room

once her soul
sheds her brass body
with a quicksilver tear

and if in fact
she will like sitting
fingers threaded

in boxy air
imagining others
pent adjacently

decorously walled
folded on themselves
stainless vesture

given that the life
for which she was made
was all about hills

bushes black with rain
sopping tresses
ewes pinned in thorn

and sky
lots of sky
and never a room

save the farmer's
of an evening
ale and repletion

candle-fire
miles away
over bony grass

from where she dealt
with blood
with real lambs dying

Come to pass

He has hollowed the cellar
till the mortar ledges out
like steps to a decommissioned heaven

crates of imperishables
look on each other
forward commanders keeping a steel-grey faith

a creviced box
hides silver, gold, tumbles of yen and zloty —

who knows what stake will win
once the world folds into its last imperturbable sickness?

books on growing veg in grave-deep mulch
on teasing warmth from pinholes

lie open on duvets under plastic
breviaries to be reverenced
when sores bud thick on the skin of the age

in the street
he keeps his nose up for the odours
on the wind after next

car cuts in, man shoves round man—
tidings of night-fires
of calamity taking snaps of itself
in a surging line of visors

'Closing Down'
runs everywhere beside him —

the arse-end of a nursery rhyme
cut loose from cockle-shell and bonnet

the imperishables were tricky to come by:
blueblood and pinstripe are deep in the game

each one night nearer
he revolves down below

casts a captain's eye
over crate, book, duvet

spreads metal and coin
so they make an unbustable flush

shivers nonetheless
as a breaching chill of new weather

finds his ribs, collarbone
his tenderly defenceless neck

The Little Sweep

Coseley 1961

it was Easter
I was seven
The Little Sweep
was due at ten-thirty
on that cough
of Rediffusion
called children's tv

but mother
had a call-out
a patient in Havacre Lane
so what I watched with her instead
was rain on her Standard's windscreen
a speeding coal-truck
a cat one life down
then (left to myself
strapped in like a madman)
old blokes
called Jabez and Horace
most likely
stuttering off
to the Deepfields train

while she was behind strange walls
clunking the metals you needed
to brew insulin
or shaking her head with brisk softness
at spina bifida
tight-lipped and exotic on its bed

when we got back
the sweep was gone
with his brushy stuff
beyond where transmitters
wave and fizzle
and the afternoon had a dirty great mouth
and dad had hidden the Dansette's plug
and I didn't like reading

still the rain though
going at the kerbstones
watched from an upstairs curtain-end
neutralising all the kids
cleansing the bone-windowed crescent

sometimes back then
heaven got out of its picture-books
and blessed easy

Unchild

Good. Annabel has found her bag.
Each day, somehow,
it flies from her shoulder
and hides hereabouts

in this dark bit
by the Year 1 door
where the Romans used to sneer down
before the Celts took over.

At lunchtime
and at the last bell
she sweeps along after it,
elbowing the dust-and-polish air

Ellie and Mona in shrill attendance,
admonition nipping her ear
from the world she has to crane up at:
I expect, silly girl, it's where you left it ...

Always she finds it here.
Always it is at my feet.
I'd lift it for her if I could.
Once she fell right through me.

I was unborn in the very same year
which makes me exactly not their age
my face is unfreckled
by all the summers that didn't see me running.

My hair is unimaginably blonde
its curls brush where my collar isn't.
I tend when standing to take my weight
on a leg boned with stillness.

The enfolding of two
cut as in mid-lovecry
by a third who urged his rights
from the depths of his violence —

that's what got me unstarted
ungrew me up healthy,
tallish, really,
for what is not my age.

But I live by my own reckoning
on sun-worried motes.
The two of them loved
and that was enough

to make me though not
to send me here
when I came not of age
to the dark bit

by the Year 1 door
where the Romans used to sneer down
before the Celts took over.
And now Annabel swings up her bag

and unknowing splits
what is not my heart
and the words from the world
she has to crane up at

echo behind her
as sweet for me as a mother's chiding,
a father's mock-bewilderment:
You'd lose your noggin if it wasn't screwed on ...

little old man

little old man
on the street
little old man
go your way

as each step of your day
dissolves another face
turns another figure inland
from the long shore of your past

as the wind
funs with your bones
if none of the young and uncaring
are available to do the same

you watch each morning
come for you
as a gunner might squint
through ruinous glass

but you have no gun
and the world stays
blue and indifferent
if it knew your last hour

it simply couldn't say
which bulking cloud
which raindrop
it hunkers in

little old man
sometimes
you can yet
stand clear of your life

be a straight-backed ghost
looking down
as if at the last sleeper
on a night-bus

but most times you are a wall
so tired
so slack
a feather-nudge from the earth

a corner turns past you
at its usual time
on you come

stiffen against
the ancient greed
of your heart and breath

you get nearer
close upon me
sigh as you climb inside

I breathe from my boots
I pulse like swung canvas
clipping a sawdust floor
I go my way

help the lonely

to be on the safe side
he took an earlier train
found the meeting cancelled
a memo pad note
stuck to the lych-gate

he stands on the platform
in an edge of country station
life smoky-distant behind him
an evening piled hugely in front

*****

she almost sort of made it
just the one drench
between the bus stop and her door
her coat slid down
dog-tired also
got itself all hem and ruckle
about the bannister post

for a good few minutes
she stands
lets the warm
fall through the day it's been
before hearing
stair by stair
room by room
the house as it starts not to talk

*****

for the sake of the afternoon
the couple loosed their children down the beach
sat adjacent
watched the shock-haired yells
in their shapeless migration
from pool to shingle to tide

babysitter next weekend
she thinks
there's that film on
two whole hours
of others catching as they can
their own hot-potato days

she cries to them
not to get too close
he turns with his first word selected
and breaks her heart

*****

the patch of sand
still bears the slewed caper
of feet big and small
toe to toe here
there the tiniest pelting away
to the dunes' lush dessication
a perfunctory breeze is still silvered
with all that tears can do

nothing more loyal
than house-warmth
after a raining street
also nothing beyond

he remembers
on a corner of the lych note
someone had written
his very name and number
easily overlooked of course
that's pencil for you

birds tack . . .

birds tack
between the spits and spots
tuck themselves

in dryish spaces
junctions of bark
farragoes of ivy

the day attempts
to remember itself
in needled pools

will have to wait
till clouds are again the ripe wax
of rain inside rain

the day's notion
of its face
is always one downpour behind

a bird's wing
is never quite dry
when next it spreads upon the thunder

*****
now the cat
flap-hustling
wet as foolery

all the sky
mad to get past
punting its haunches

flap down
cat dead out at all four corners
unable to credit

the inebriate rain
the bird-theft
the summer

appalling the windows
huffing the walls
hind-legged like the beast
it can never be

The Gather-man

In certain cultures, the gather-man prepares the soon-to-die. He is not, however, in death's direct employment. Nor is it his business to speak of heaven, hell or their local equivalents.

1

The gather-man

The gather-man sits
on his own side of the afternoon

leans me a smile across the table
raises demurring hands against another cup

his palms are steady as the cold
that pools under winter bridges
his eyes are garnet-bright

since he came
the days have fallen like snow

I accept it:
he is the watcher of low candles
we are preparing

there is a road between right this minute
my fingers telling the rounded heat of tea

and the fields of last panic
orphan words
my little stinks of terror

the gather-man says
he doesn't know it in miles
I don't dare not believe him.

Yesterday
he got me used to shadows —
they fear, too, must reach for their kind

showed me how lush they lie
about church porches
in sun-provoked lanes

let me hear their chatter
as they are swayed down
cartooning their ignorant owners

and there was a girl
crutch-swung

failing against the town's hill
pushing at last through a little door up top

the gather-man told
of her chair and cup, her single drawer

how echo-nests are strawed within her beams
how the hours pile fatly about her

the message tape for her phone
stays bubbled and sealed

but weather or wind
she comes half-stilting down

feet out and over the morning
a child on a carney wheel

lands in a line at the market street
dips among the roses and roses

coaxes the day into yielding up
a fresh hand of remembrance.

The gather-man leans again
brackets my fingers

tomorrow he will adjust me
to how peaks and fells live their silence
the tale of the willow's weep

now we are eye to eye
his everlasting
folds about my sputter

learn, he says,
learn that girl

Something of that

Something of that
says my fallowed heart
when I picture the hour
after it resigns me

my spirit, it says,
will not be fingered
by one or other claimant
in a scissoring of light

waiting needs width
flooring to gaze on
room for prayer and disbelief
and dumbness to play tag

so I picture my old school
the glass-ushered corridor
science labs to library
it is Friday

October, an old-gold afternoon
I look down at friends
full-tilt in a local fixture
on the tiring field

when they drop back
the dusk eats into their bodies
they become what a bee would buzz
if the sound were yellow and grey

I picture all the kids to come
marching from the labs in hand-pressed colours
all the kids gone
powdered through the library door

my two claimants emerge
from the hill behind the goalposts
stroll abreast along the touchline
boulevardiers with a day to break in on

one stills the run of play
which the other restores —
power like an old joke:
the way, I guess, you tell it

they enter below where I wait
I become the song of the mayfly
all knowing and unknowing furled
in a single throw of moments

only one of them ascending the stairs

the gather-man squeezes my shoulder
wishes me sweet dreams of hayfields
in a summer with nothing to prove

3

his Chatterton is remarkable

The gather-man and I
play farewells

his Chatterton is remarkable
hanging south-west off the sofa

all those iambics flowing to his head
hand ricked as if to catch one heartbeat
poke it back under his blouse

I am a strongman
who rose from the furrows to arrogate a throne
made of blades and signatures, smiles in the midnight

at stately peace now
filed past by a people
who never got to see their lives
but will say soon enough
that at least you knew where you were

the gather-man obliges
walks between wall and wall
with a bag of blorts and snuffles

souring the held breath
of a palace where even the motes
fear to dance

he's as giddy a goat as me —
with his red slide down a Chicago wall
streaks arrowing up
to where his last breath and cologne still hang

in turn I give him my chappie of means
all of a suddenly dropsical pickle
rag-dolling down the Spanish Steps

and am just readying
my Pitt the Younger

when he falls, bloats, livers up
unzips his neck
to free a neap tide of rats and backswimmers

evacuates like a twilit ruminant
causes a lake to bruise over the side he dresses

keeps a moon eye upon me
as, neatly unfragmenting, he swings to his feet

I forgo Pitt
Little Nell
the poet who clambered down sixteen wooded rhymes
and filled up with snow

4

lau-

Towards dawn I get frightened again
my eyes can't open or close
the gather-man reaches
his hand takes me across busy roads
for an evening love-walk
hauls me over a tailgate
gingers all my personal belongings
between the train and the platform's edge
dances me clockwise
threads me out of the circles
till I'm the furthest away
from the couple in the middle
footing it under the lych-roof of arms
bursting
flowing their road out from under their step

a road
I maybe, maybe don't cry
remembering a cousin an uncle and me
coming from a bar
late summer early yellows
someone else with uncle
cap, twine, the smell of a year tough enough
road fall road bend

. . . the gather-man's hand staying put then withdrawing . . .

cousin and me in step
still road
he says I say he embroiders I snort
laughter laughter laughter
lau-

Shelter Poems

in their quiet

In the first of the morning
when the hour still holds its rose
there's nothing more lovely
than staring at things in their quiet

a vase on the kitchen counter
candles impressed with a robin
flown clear of its mortal Christmas
the blind softening all to shadow on a rested stream

things in their quiet think no harm
don't cup the heart in bloodless fingers
ask neither belief nor promise
nor tears when dark's at the full

they belong in first morning
even forgive time's will to grow
when the afternoon loud and unwiped comes on
the sun unspeakably fattens

morning and quiet are the only kingdom
I stand with the vase
the candles
try to live as they do
catch fleetingly their secret

as a coat catches winter
hides it soft and brief indoors
is forced to feel it die
in the house's oblivious weather

proddable all over

With thanks and acknowledgement to Simon, Burton-on-Trent Quest Writers' Group, for suggesting this poem's theme.

Sense
yes, it makes sense to me
though the doctor was bent up in agony
shuffling papers he'd aimed at the bin
swooping his computer-mouse
across that mat of his that chirrups
We're all a bit mad
talking head-down
like my eyes had decamped to his knuckles
coming out at last with a wheezy blurt:
Thing is, we've had the results back
Thing is, you're not real

perfect sense
now I see why people walk through me on the street
why shop assistants look round and over and under me
then reckon there's no-one to serve
the bell must have clanged out of boredom
and disappear into their soft furnishings
hamper pyramids
must-have tents and gazebos

now I know
why the postman brakes and swivels
at my gate
treks off with his yeoman's weight
of good-bad rainy-sunny news
to drop into others' mornings
people you can see
whose height and girth
could be trapped in any measure
people you could prod
who make noises that are their names and lives

he's good, the doctor
means well
says *how are you? not how are we?*

which in its odd little quaint little way
makes a difference I can't find the words for

so it pains me to challenge, to disprove
I wasn't brought up like that

but I'm real enough
an onion will melt my eyes
nylon will rash up my skin
like a pink-knotted tree a child might draw
when it's fresh out of limes or umbers
I can find seals and marmosets
in the scrambling climb of clouds in August
I'd give you what you'd expect
if you held my hand over a blossoming flame
or dropped strawberries into my lap

The world makes me laugh, cry
and tickle my chin
like you do
tent-and-gazebo seller
swivelling postman
people who lend their names to morning envelopes
whose height and girth are statistically blunt
are proddable all over

next time in the surgery
I'll take doctor's hand
say *how are you?* not *we?*
pump it up and down
to the tick of his lotion-advertisement clock
greeting and zest
and bone-pure humanity
will flow from my palm into his
I'll get him drunk on salutation
give him all the *hail fellow* he could stand
from pills-rep, double-glazer, son-in-law combined
all the real he'll ever need
in this life
the next
the uncountable afters

how far are they fallen?

I've never liked keys
they sadden space

trap the body
its fields and sunstrikes

in coffin-sketch frames
only for a moment perhaps

but one taste of prisoning
forever dyes the breath

anyone with keys must go on and on
wrong ones diminish them

right ones abrade their fingers
once they're lost in their damp little joy

and all the while a letter lies unbegun
a good deed planned flitters down beneath old leaves

keys free nothing
but the scent of acts departed

shrink curiosity to a gleam
sloughed by the sun

and when they are done these key-folk
how far are they fallen from themselves?

on what blank-skimming ledge
must they sideways their feet?

keys face forward only
pay out no homing thread

mine stay put
between the hook and their curlicues
a spider has woven me
buds of snow

those pens asleep

look at those pens asleep
no words fret them now
time is dried in their barrels

they no longer speak a certain heart
let's say
shed its bewilderment and fear
on mats in clock-sedated hallways

don't as it might be induce
the collapse of love in middle years

so he sees and doesn't see
how rain on shop windows
breaks his face

so she stands in each day
as a woman might in an empty square
turns   calls   stands again
echo shawling her arms

while even those caught lone for now
beside him at the window
in the next square along
know how to thread their way
have a prophecy of other hands
plumping the home
shooing off the night

the pens lean anyhow in their pot
as spring might happen
by a tree bole on an unknown path

lazing clash-colour heads
my flowers

Exits

I didn't mean it!

rain

door
voice
dog
voice
dogs
slap
voice
punch
cry
gate
voice
slam
car
scream
revs
grind
fade

sobs

bird

sobs

rain

Over

Again you brace yourself
for a life of Sundays.
Back comes the depleting need
to not think.

The gap
between skull and mind
fills with predictions
of headache.

Sometimes it's the chafe
of a roughly-hitched belt
in there. Sometimes
it's just cold.

You move down one.
Bouncing back
is tougher to lie. Anyway,
you're older: what's to bounce?

You walk in parks,
under suns you have come to despise.
Passing couples rake you
with laughter, with beginnings.

You can't manage
a full straight sentence. To try
is like shaping ramparts in childhood mash —
still the gravy cleaves in.

Hate gets its other hand
onto the rungs. You see a pretty face
and your fingers dive, pretend to curl
round what isn't deep in your bag.

At each day's end
you hurry off into yourself—
but find yourself doesn't know who you are
and anyway can't spare the shelter.

The Flipside
'Space Oddity'

They even got my name wrong
canyouhearmeMajorTom?
canyouhearme?
their voices dervishing
the last bees of summer
bottomed in a jar

the trouble I've spared them ...
hours like years of balls in mouth
the molten ballyhoo of re-entry
all those tv screens worldwide
belly-up in the Pacific

plus the President
I hear
has a charnel grip —
no way to firm a handshake
between star and lump

canyouhear? canyoucanyou?
bad gas from the underworld
my circuits are very much alive
will sing me out
sing out planet earth
which
last I looked
had the skin of a tomb
when the may grass rises

I shall pad off
across creation's taut muslin
tomorrow I broach my hundredth galaxy
with the demoleculated scotch
I smuggled on

I have hearts to touch down in
burning paws to clasp
hugs to tendril into
no colour all colour ridges to crest

worlds to save worth the saving

This is the best

This is the best
of an afternoon
pillow warm to my face
a push at the calves
where the rug is folded half over
far below the window the world
its chipper nothings

all the parades have gone
I caught the litter-sticker's last grumble
what forests in the stillness
what oceans
branch and latitude keeping mum

right side is better
it brings back the pictures worth smoothing
a twin-set lady when I was eight
prayer-cards and a spray of rosaries
tapping over the tracks between the boat-trains
St Paul's work freshly in hand
amid the damnations of Crewe

a Cutty Sark ashtray
a tree-bole pot
remaindered on the door-ledge
for the lawless tip
how they got forgotten
how I hid them at last and gave them names
readied them in my head each night
to go hand in lovely implausible hand
down a moon-braided road
to a land that smelt of kisses and cedar
and wasn't this

left side will do
but it pops out the ear plugs
plus I'm facing the window
the curtains are folded as deep
as how I once heard love described

but why risk?
hearts are flensed out there
street and parish struggle hot
bombs do for the innards of life
though people's eyes are still a cow-child's
though they look each new day up and down
and say ah now this one
this gift will give

and that other picture
the time just after college
when I saw an aunt off on a train
and caught swimmer's ear from her homilies
that sounded the way furtive corduroy smells
and shook them out of my head

and found my way home
was a dream of forks and crossings
but no knuckles pressing *thisaway* into my back
no purpose waxing like an uncle's Christmas fart

last day of summer
I should have just stood forever
between say the churchyard
and that funny old sway-about wall
let the dusks and the moons and the dews
come on in their way
old snowflake old sol
geese and cuckoo

just stood like now lying here
pillow rug curtain fold
love with all its peril surrendered
fastness
keep

Terraplane

I could mention I saw a bat
that it cut and poured evening onto its wing
jumped the quarries of air
ran its lanes like a country mortician
called late to the back of beyond
clattering on his black waistcoat

that it made colour lose its nerve
pinned fence to branch to stone
dragged the night from inside them

lay easy a moment
on nothing
imprinting masteries of jack and dive
for hunter-birds to recover
all over again at first light

a terraplane
I could call it
shucking carriageway dirt
from its underplates
rising
to where the placemen of creation
sit on clouds
weigh their measured heaps
of anger, wind, calamity
then flip their palms
loosing each at its human mark

terraplane
I almost say
almost turning
to the lightless walls of the house

but she strides unhearing
tightens a line of inventory
with each twist of the keys on her finger

soon she'll be gone
strewing pictures of us
from an uncommitting hand
soon after
the rooms will be tanks of echo
squared hard round finality

tomorrow night
there'll be the windows only
no-one to see them seeing
that bear the wide fidget of ivy
catch maybe a single loop of a bat
and forget

waiting for rain and leaf-ghosts
to fuss at the back of new lives

Uninsured

Heaven's eye takes pictures
the street was never graded to bear:
a lagoon enchantment,
figures lolling astern,
trailing a fear apiece like hands
in an August bay.

Lily-pads wheel over suck-holes,
play doorsteppers,
play crown-the-lintel.

Upstairs, a terrace of life
is dry a touch longer.

Keepsakes hold their story
inches apart,
knowing their shapes
by the shapes they are not,
respecting how each other
fell off the back of affection
into evermores of dust.

Upstairs is still summer,
a proffered kiss,
a bad calculation
evened with courteous regret.

Downstairs is unmaking.
Bolts are away like minnows
from a wafering hulk;
glue sighs thanks
that its clench of dowel and mortise
is revoked.

Plates, coasters are deepwater eyes
bleared with electrics,
the oak-smoke of irregular flex,
the pilot-light's tango,
the nine, eight, seven before all hell.

Shannon

dark channel
thick weather
weak signal
no headland
cars grating
dogs whining
bar bursting
sky melting
hunched lookout
doused starboard
clouds laughing
kids asking
kids whining
kids crying
dogs rolling
cars melting
air bursting

black channel
no lookout
no signal

Union Junction

Napton Pride
nods to Flower of Glasnevin

paint-embroidered cans hang portside
awaiting Victorian rain

buffer tyres ride the basin water
undulations in a toy Loch Ness

The Light of Bewdley hasn't been tended
lows like a cow full of ironbound milk

masts tilt and parry mid-basin
each with the direst journey to tell

a single swan
the sun's approbation prinking its neck

sails into the midst of it all
arresting the braggart clack of the masts
stilling The Light of Bewdley
going wide about for Upper Gilgal Bridge

a bike-boy on the marina
watches as it fashions its wake
of gusted leaves and coots and water-boatmen

as a child might stand
moon-eyed
quiver-mouthed
while eternity
with patient smile
explains itself

Last Poem

On a Thursday afternoon
with the roads and the gardens
full of nearly rain
the final word gives in
and takes its place

such an ill-sorted word
for that moment
a morning-flower word
an eye bright already
in the minute before dawn
a word to start a holiday
to blow about
a bride's step-frothing train
a yes in its own circle-song

but there nonetheless
in a poem that clangs the door
that is the back view
of a trilby'd man with a suitcase
on a smoke-baffled platform
as the porter draws the gate
on the late express
that is the arranging handshake
of old friends who part for home
one to stamp feet on the porch-mat
the other to die in the dark

a word running this way
in a poem running that

and the pages lie as left
the pen sleeps capless
on a road and garden Thursday
with rain just begun

Oversteps Books Ltd

The Oversteps list includes books by the following poets:

David Grubb, Giles Goodland, Alex Smith, Will Daunt, Patricia Bishop, Christopher Cook, Jan Farquarson, Charles Hadfield, Mandy Pannett, Doris Hulme, James Cole, Helen Kitson, Bill Headdon, Avril Bruton, Marianne Larsen, Anne Lewis-Smith, Mary Maher, Genista Lewes, Miriam Darlington, Anne Born, Glen Phillips, Rebecca Gethin, W H Petty, Melanie Penycate, Andrew Nightingale, Caroline Carver, John Stuart, Ann Segrave, Rose Cook, Jenny Hope, Hilary Elfick, Jennie Osborne, Anne Stewart, Oz Hardwick, Angela Stoner, Terry Gifford, Michael Swan, Denise Bennett, Maggie Butt, Anthony Watts, Joan McGavin, Robert Stein, Graham High, Ross Cogan, Ann Kelley, A C Clarke, Diane Tang, Susan Taylor, R V Bailey, John Daniel, Alwyn Marriage, Simon Williams, Kathleen Kummer, Jean Atkin, Charles Bennett, Elisabeth Rowe, Marie Marshall, Ken Head, Robert Cole, Cora Greenhill, John Torrance, Michael Bayley, Christopher North, Simon Richey, Lynn Roberts, Sue Davies and Mark Totterdell.

For details of all these books, information about Oversteps and up-to-date news, please look at our website:

www.overstepsbooks.com